IBN SINA

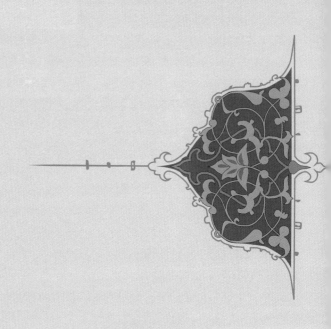

Ibn Sina

A CONCISE LIFE

Edoardo Albert

KUBE
PUBLISHING

To Harriett, Theodore,
Matthew and Isaac

Ibn Sina: A concise life

First published in England by Kube Publishing Ltd,
Markfield Conference Centre, Ratby Lane, Markfield,
Leicestershire LE67 9SY, United Kingdom
Tel: +44 (0) 1530 249230
Fax: +44 (0) 1530 249656
Website: www.kubepublishing.com
Email: info@kubepublishing.com

Design, typesetting, maps, patterns: Louis Mackay
Editor: Yosef Smyth

Every effort has been made to trace and acknowledge ownership of copyright. The
publishers offer to rectify any omissions in future editions, following notification.

A Cataloguing-in-Publication Data record for this
Book is available from the British Library

ISBN 978-1-84774-045-8 paperback

Printed by Imak Ofset, Turkey

Contents

Maps

Illustrations

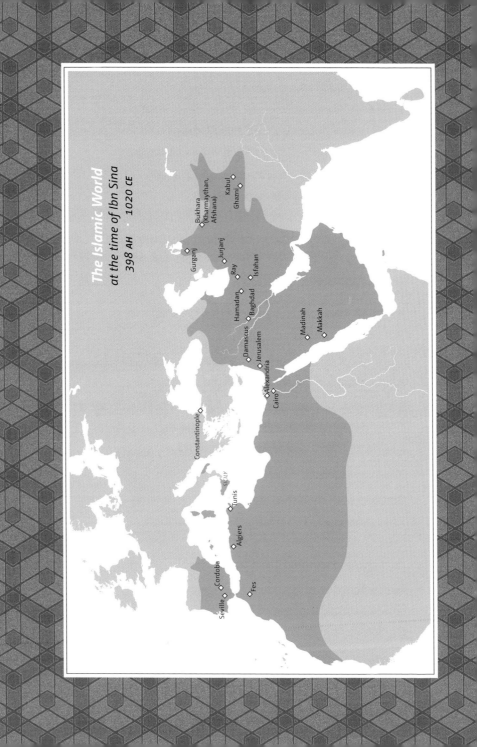

The Islamic World
at the time of Ibn Sina
398 AH · 1020 CE

Gurganj
Jurjanj
Bukhara (Kharmaythan, Afshana)
Kabul
Ghazni
Ray
Isfahan
Hamadan
Baghdad
Madinah
Makkah
Damascus
Jerusalem
Alexandria
Cairo
Constantinople
SICILY
Tunis
Algiers
Seville
Cordoba
Fes

Who was Ibn Sina?

Ibn Sina was a doctor, a philosopher, an astronomer, a mathematician, a logician, a grammarian, a politician, a poet and a traveller – and he was possibly the last man to know everything. Today, it is impossible for any one person to know everything, but a little over a thousand years ago, when Ibn Sina was born, it was just about possible for a single man to keep all the major fields of knowledge in his head. Ibn Sina mastered every subject that existed in the Islamic world of his time and, since the Islamic world had access to the knowledge of the ancient Greeks as well as the ideas coming from India and China, that meant he knew pretty well all there was to know.

But Ibn Sina's life was not dedicated to learning alone – rather it was a life full of intrigue, desperate escapes and long imprisonments, played out against a background of kingdoms crashing down and new ones clawing their way to power. For he lived at a time when the early political unity of the Islamic world had fractured and competing principalities fought to establish themselves and to overthrow older dynasties. And not only was there competition among princes, there was a conflict of ideas. For the breakneck expansion of Islam in the seventh, eighth and ninth centuries had brought a nomadic, desert-living people, the Arabs, into contact with some of the oldest and most literate civilisations in the world. Indeed, in most cases, the Arabs, by virtue of their conquests, were now in charge of these ancient civilisations. In particular, the advance of Muslim armies brought all the lands of the old Persian Empire, and much of the territory of the Greek-speaking Byzantine Empire, under the control of Arabic speaking rulers. With this expansion, there came a confrontation: what were the adherents of the new religion to make of the ideas of the ancient Greeks and Persians? In particular, Greek philosophers such as Plato and Aristotle posed a challenge to religion: could the truth about God and the universe be arrived at through rational inquiry, as the Greeks taught, and what were Muslims to make of the arguments of the philosophers that opposed tenets of their religion?

Ibn Sina was one of the first Muslims to meet this challenge head on; for him, there was no intrinsic opposition between religion and reason, and he set about reconciling the two. The philosophical synthesis he made still inspires thinkers today, as well as having a defining impact on the Muslim world of his time.

But if this sounds like Ibn Sina's main concern, think again. Ibn Sina pursued his philosophical inquiries in his own time, usually working late into the night. In order to support himself Ibn Sina worked as a physician, and it is as a doctor that he entered popular knowledge. The encyclopaedia of medicine that he wrote, the *Canon of Medicine*, became the standard medical textbook in the

An illuminated page from Ibn Sina's *Canon of Medicine*

Islamic and, after being translated, European worlds for hundreds of years. For in his book, Ibn Sina systematised the knowledge of the ancient Greeks and brought it up to date with his own extraordinary stock of medical experience and insight. Perhaps most importantly, Ibn Sina emphasised the need for good hygiene when treating a patient. Indeed, so great was his reputation among ordinary people that, after his death, Ibn Sina entered folklore and became a byword as a magician and sorcerer.

In the west, Ibn Sina was known as Avicenna, after the Latinised version of his name. And as Avicenna, he became for centuries the foremost medical authority in European universities, the *Canon of Medicine* being used to train generations of doctors.

The way that extraordinary stories clustered around Ibn Sina indicates another facet of his life: he apparently had absolutely no regard for what other people thought of him. It was easy to gossip about Ibn Sina because he gave rumour-mongers a great deal of material with which to attack him – his fondness for late-night social gatherings was notorious. However, Ibn Sina's enemies, and he had many enemies both during his life and afterwards, embellished the rumours with all sort of scurrilous stories, until in folk tradition Ibn Sina became known as a magician. But the fact that the mud stuck showed how scandalous a figure he sometimes cut in contemporary society. As such, the life of Ibn Sina shows us that the early medieval Islamic world was much more varied and complex than it is usually portrayed.

Since Ibn Sina spent most of his life travelling from the court of one ruler to another, an examination of his life also takes us into many different parts of the Islamic world of his time. After all, he left his homeland at the age of twenty-two and never returned. At the end of his life, Ibn Sina famously said, "I prefer a short life with width to a narrow one with length." He had his wish.

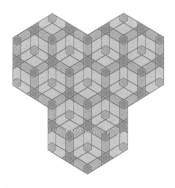

The Samanid
Mausoleum in
Bukhara. Built
in the 10th
Century CE.

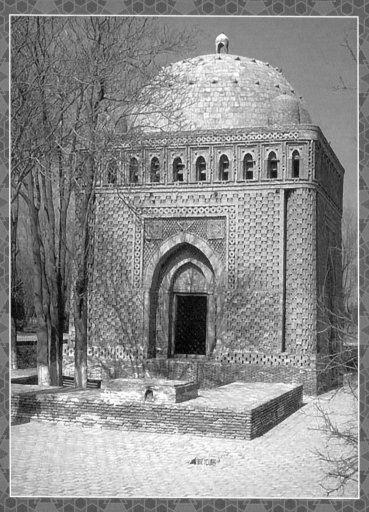

CHAPTER 1

Childhood

Ibn Sina was born in August 980 (Safar 370) in a village called Afshana near the city of Bukhara, which lies in the present-day country of Uzbekistan in central Asia. His full name was Abu Ali Al-Husain ibn Abd-Allah ibn Hasan ibn Ali ibn Sina – the name is so long because it includes the names of his father, grandfather and great grandfather – but it was as Ibn Sina that he became known to the Islamic world. His father was an official of the Samanids, a powerful dynasty in Iran and Uzbekistan at the time, and one of sufficiently high rank to be trusted with the governorship of the town of Kharmaythan and its surrounding villages, including Afshana, by the **amir**. It was while he was living in Afshana that he met and married the woman who was to be Ibn Sina's mother. She was called Sitara and, five years after Ibn Sina was born, she gave birth to his younger brother, Mahmud. Mahmud was later to prove a faithful brother and companion to Ibn Sina through many years of exile.

The Samanids were originally given provinces by the Abbasid Caliph al-Mamun, in reward for their service to him. But in a time when a message to the court of the Caliph in Baghdad could take weeks to arrive, the

Samanids became increasingly autonomous. However, the Samanids always styled themselves as amirs, that is governors, and their coinage always bore the Caliph's name.

The area where Ibn Sina was born and grew up was at the crossroads between China, India and the Islamic world, and people of many different backgrounds lived there. It seems most likely that Ibn Sina was Persian, born of Persian parents, particularly as his mother's name means 'star' in that language.

Shortly after Mahmud's birth, the family moved back to Bukhara. The city was the capital of the Samanids, who had made it a graceful and prosperous town. Bukhara lies on the banks of the River Zarashan in the country that is today Uzbekistan. Bukhara is a long way from the sea, on the edge of the great plains of Central Asia, in a harsh land, consisting mainly of mid-altitude desert. These plains, or steppes, were the ancestral homelands of tribes of nomadic pastoralists, who made their living by herding their animals across the steppes to where they could find grazing during fiercely hot summers, and shelter through bitterly cold winters. It was a tough life and the tribesmen were tough people, who spent a great deal of time fighting each other. However, if a warlord could unite the tribes then the resulting army was often unstoppable.

A century and a half after Ibn Sina, the greatest and most terrible of these warlords, Genghis Khan, would sweep down from the steppes and bring a crashing,

Bukhara

There have been people living in the region of Bukhara for thousands of years, but the city enters written history around about 500BCE. Owing to its position on the Silk Road and the water that allowed travelling caravans to refresh themselves on their long trade journeys, it became a major town. When the Samanids made Bukhara the capital of their dynasty, it grew larger still, with a central fortress, a town centre to the west of the fortress, and suburbs protected by high walls. Advanced hydrological engineering meant that water was brought from the river into the city, with covered reservoirs built alongside the roads the caravans used to allow merchants and their animals to drink.

blood-stained end to the golden age of the Islamic world. But, for now, the walls the Samanids had built around Bukhara were enough to stop the small bands of raiders who came up against the city. More often, however, the nomads came to trade, for Bukhara lay on the Silk Road.

A trading caravan on the Silk Road, in a medieval Catalan atlas.

The Silk Road was the name for the overland trading routes that connected China and India with Europe and the Middle East. As the name indicates, silk was one of the main products traded along the route. The Chinese had discovered how to weave silk from the secretions of the mulberry silkworm as long ago as 3,500 BCE, but the Emperors of China tried to reserve the secret of silk manufacture to themselves and for thousands of years silk cloth could only be obtained by trading with the Chinese. Since silk was a highly prized and very expensive cloth, it became worthwhile for traders to make the long and hazardous journey across Asia to China for the silk, before returning home. Large-scale trade in silk and other luxury items began in the first century BCE, and grew as the appetite of the Romans for the exotic material fostered trade. And even when Rome fell, the continuing Byzantine Empire and the expanding Islamic world provided flourishing markets for trade. A town, such as Bukhara, lying on the Silk Road profited greatly from the caravans passing through, from east to west and back again.

Even before the family moved back to Bukhara, there were signs that Ibn Sina was unusually intelligent. According to one story, the infant Ibn Sina heard his mother bewailing the loss of a beautiful and valuable necklace. But he was so young that, although he understood what Sitarah was saying, he did not have enough language to tell her where to look; for he had seen her put the necklace down. However, as Ibn Sina grew a little older, and learned how to speak, he remembered his mother's lost necklace and told her where to find it.

As the Samanid capital, and with its position on the Silk Road, Bukhara provided a much more cosmopolitan environment in which to grow up than Afshana. It also offered teachers – and Ibn Sina's parents had, by this time, realised that their precocious elder son wanted and needed to learn.

Ibn Sina's early education followed the traditional pattern: study of the Qur'an, which also involved memorising as much of the text as the learner found possible, and learning the literature of Persia and Arabia, with some Indian and Greek stories too.

As a child, Ibn Sina would either have visited his teacher at his house, or met him at the mosque, where the teacher would sit, with his students gathered cross-legged around him, while he went through the texts and the pupils learned what he said by rote. If this seems a boring way of learning, remember that books were rare and precious objects in Ibn Sina's day. Thus, for most people, learning something meant committing it to memory.

Children at madrasah in an ancient Persian manuscript.

This early learning served Ibn Sina well, for it trained his memory, and in his years of wandering often all he could take with him was his memory of books he knew, the books themselves having been lost or stolen.

In his own words

" I was put under teachers of the Qur'an and of letters. By the time I was ten I had mastered the Qur'an and a great deal of literature, so that I was marvelled at for my aptitude. "

These words are Ibn Sina's own. Unusually for a man of his time, as an adult Ibn Sina dictated a short autobiography to one of his faithful pupils, telling the story of his life up until that time. That pupil, Abu Ubayd al-Juzjani, later wrote down an account of the rest of Ibn Sina's life, during the many years when he accompanied his master. But memorising the Qur'an was just the start of Ibn Sina's education (to get an idea of how big an achievement that was for a ten-year-old boy, a typical English translation of the Qur'an is over 400 pages long).

For many children of the time, formal education would have stopped at this point, but Ibn Sina's father had the money to educate his son further. Ibn Sina went on to learn **shari'ah** (Islamic law) and **fiqh**, that is Islamic jurisprudence. Of all topics, this was the most important building block for a career as a scholar in the Islamic world of Ibn Sina's time. Fiqh is necessary because, while the Qur'an gives clear instructions to believers in many matters, there are other areas upon which it is silent. The next step is to study what the Prophet Muhammad

A discussion in a village, from a 13th Century CE manuscript.

did and taught, the **Sunnah**. But if both are silent, then a combination of reasoning and consensus has to be employed, and this is where the study of fiqh comes in.

Having put the fundamentals in place, Ibn Sina's father was determined to educate his bright son further and he sent the boy to learn mathematics with "a certain vegetable-seller who used the Indian arithmetic". This was a revolutionary way of doing mathematics because finger counting was the normal method of calculation at that time.

'Indian arithmetic' is the basis of the way we do mathematics today. It involved an entirely new way of representing numbers, replacing the finger counting that Ibn Sina also learned, and the Roman-style numerals that were widely used. The system was first developed in India around 500 CE. First came individual characters to represent the numbers one to nine, and then the crucial invention of the zero. These nine simple numbers and zero allowed huge numbers to be written down easily and quickly. For instance, compare 8,748 with its Roman equivalent: MMMMMMMMDCCXLVIII. They also allowed people to calculate accurately and quickly on paper.

Counting with fingers

Counting with fingers, which is called **dactylonomy**, is much more than just counting to ten. The fingers have three bones, two joints and a knuckle, and using them in combination it was possible to count to 9,999. The Arabs called it 'the arithmetic of the knots (finger joints)' and many people preferred it because it required only your body: no paper, pen, abacus or counters. Ibn Sina was skilled in this type of counting too, for he invented a better form of it many years later, when he was 49.

The superiority of this system of numbering meant that it started spreading out from India almost as soon as it was developed. For example, a Christian bishop who lived in Syria in 662 CE wrote:

> I will omit all discussion of the science of the Indians ... of their subtle discoveries in astronomy, discoveries that are more ingenious than those of the Greeks and the Babylonians, and of their valuable methods of calculation which surpass description. I wish only to say that this computation is done by means of nine signs. If those who believe, because they speak Greek, that they have arrived at the limits of science, would read the Indian texts, they would be convinced, even if a little late in the day, that there are others who know something of value.

But it was the Arabs who adopted and spread the new numbers most widely. In Arabic-speaking countries, the numbers are still called 'Indian' to this day. The spread of Islam meant that scholars could communicate with each other in Arabic over huge distances, and one of their foremost topics was mathematics. Two great scholars, Al-Khwarizmi and Al-Kindi, wrote guides to using the new numbers in the early ninth century. But it was only in the twelfth century that their works were translated into Latin, and then into other European languages. Over the next two hundred years, this 'Arabic' system of numbering took over from the Roman one in Europe, a process that was hastened by the invention of the printing press in 1454. Since then, these nine numbers and zero have gone on to become the most universal language in the world, one that is used by people everywhere.

Ibn Sina would go on to make some notable contributions to astronomy, for which his early learning of the new mathematics served him well, but his greatest renown came in the field to which his next teacher introduced him: philosophy.

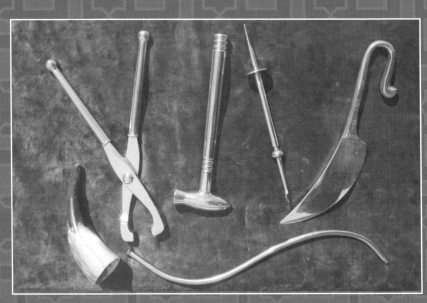

Medical instruments of the type Ibn Sina
would have used in treating patients.

CHAPTER 2

The young prodigy

Ever keen to educate his young prodigy further, Ibn Sina's father engaged another teacher. Abu Abd Allah al-Natili was a travelling scholar who knew philosophy. Ibn Sina was now moving beyond the normal curriculum of the time into the exciting, and sometimes dangerous, currents of ideas unleashed by the encounter of the Islamic and Classical worlds.

In his own words

" *Then there came to Bukhara a man called Abu Abd Allah al-Natili who claimed to be a philosopher; my father invited him to stay in our house, hoping that I would learn from him also ... He marvelled at me exceedingly, and warned my father that I should not engage in any other occupation but learning.* **"**

Beyond his wish to stretch his son, there may have been another factor behind Ibn Sina's father's decision to have him taught philosophy: religion. For Ibn Sina's father became interested in, and possibly embraced, the teachings of the Ismaili branch of Islam, and one of its key methods of gaining converts was through philosophical discussions.

Ismailism

Ismailis are a sect of Shia Muslims, that is, one of the groups that have split off from the majority, Sunni interpretation of Islam. At the time that Ibn Sina lived, the rulers of Egypt were Ismailis. The Fatimids, as they were called, were a dynasty of warriors who came originally from what was then called Ifriqiya, after its name when it was a province of Rome, and is now called Tunisia and Algeria. They had conquered the countries of north Africa from Morocco all the way to Egypt, and carried on east into the countries that are today Israel, Lebanon and Syria. The ruler of the Fatimid Dynasty was called the caliph and was regarded as the rightful ruler of the whole Islamic world by Ismailis. This put the Fatimid Dynasty in direct opposition to the caliphs who ruled in Baghdad, the rival centre of power at the time. These caliphs were the head of the Abbasid Dynasty (750 CE to 1258 CE). As part of their overriding aim to claim the leadership of the Islamic world, the Fatimids organised a network of missionaries and, in effect, secret agents, whose task it was to infiltrate the countries under the rule of the Abbasids and there to preach the doctrine of the Ismailis to win converts to their cause, and to work to undermine and overthrow the rulers of those countries.

Fatamid coin and (above) minarets of Al-Azhar, Egypt, founded in 970CE.

The Fatimids ruled from 909 to 1171, and for the first two hundred years or so were both powerful and rich. At its peak, the Fatimid Dynasty controlled all of north Africa, Egypt – its power base, where the Fatimids founded the city of Cairo – and most of Syria, Jordan, Israel and Lebanon, as well as the two holy cities, Makkah and Madinah. With its network of secret missionaries and agents, the Fatimids caused something approaching panic in the Sunni-ruled part of the Muslim world; the nearest modern equivalent would be the alarm at suspected Communist secret agents that gripped the United States in the 1950s. As such, anyone living in a Sunni state suspected of having sympathies for the Ismaili cause could face various penalties, ranging from loss of position through to imprisonment and death.

" *My father was among those who listened to the message of the Egyptians and he was reckoned among the Ismaili. My father and my brother also listened to the Ismaili's ideas about the soul and the intellect. I'd hear them discussing these things, and while I comprehended what they said, my spirit would not accept it.* "

The fact that Ibn Sina's father and brother were known to be at least sympathetic to the Ismailis was to cause Ibn Sina many difficulties over the years, even though he rejected Ismaili doctrines himself. Although Ibn Sina maintains a discreet silence in his autobiography, many scholars believe that his journeys from one court to another as an adult were in part to avoid falling into the clutches of the more strictly Sunni realms in his part of the world, who might not have been kind to anyone coming from a family that supported the Ismailis.

Scholars have argued at some length over Ibn Sina's own religious beliefs. The man himself was careful not to give too much away. Perhaps this is because the true centre of his life was not religion but learning. For Ibn Sina, the claims of the intelligence always came before faith, and, while he was a religious man, his religion was founded upon his intelligence and not vice versa.

Sunni and Shia

There are two main branches of Islam: Sunni and Shia. Shia Muslims believe that the leader of the Muslim community should be a descendant of the Prophet Muhammad himself. The fourth caliph, Ali, was the son-in-law of the Prophet and he is the only one of the first four caliphs that Shia Muslims regard as legitimate – indeed, the word Shia means 'the party of Ali'.

Ibn Sina studied the cosmological works of Ptolemy, imagined below (right) with Aristotle in a 17th-century CE Italian engraving.

Sources are silent as to Abu Abd Allah al-Natili's affiliations, but he may have been one of the secret missionary agents of the Fatimids. However, the young Ibn Sina – and he was only in his early teens at the time – proved, both for the teacher and his family, impossible to persuade. He would only accept what he had himself proved through logic and reasoning.

Abu Abd Allah al-Natili began teaching his young pupil philosophy with a translation of the *Isagoge* by Porphyry (234-305). This book was the basic introduction to logic for a millennium and, as such, the perfect starting point for a mind as rigorous as Ibn Sina's.

The young Ibn Sina took to the study of logic immediately and soon surpassed his teacher, for "whatever problem he stated to me, I showed a better mental conception of it than he". With logic mastered, Ibn Sina's teacher, who must by this time have become a little wary of the young prodigy he was teaching, introduced him to geometry through the works of Euclid, and to astronomy and cosmology via Ptolemy's *Almagest*. Thus the young scholar – he was still under sixteen – was acquiring all the most advanced knowledge of his time.

The Abbasid Caliph Harun al-Rashid in a bath house, depicted in a Persian miniature.

The translators

Greek and Arabic are very different languages, with not even a shared alphabet. So translating Greek texts into Arabic was no easy task. However, Muslims were keen to appropriate new knowledge, and the task was facilitated by the enthusiastic support of the early Abbasid caliphs. In particular, the caliphs Harun al-Rashid and his son al-Mamun supported learning, with al-Mamun founding the House of Wisdom (*Bayt al-Hikma*) in Baghdad in 830 to support scholarship.

After a while, al-Natili simply passed Ibn Sina the books and told him to get on with them. This no doubt pleased his student, who could therefore carry on his studies at his own blistering pace. To be fair to al-Natili, he had done what all true teachers set out to achieve: he had made Ibn Sina into an independent learner and thinker.

In his own words

" I moved on to the Almagest; when I had finished the prolegomena and reached the geometrical figures, al-Natili told me to go on reading and to solve the problems by myself; I should merely revise what I read with him, so that he might indicate to me what was right and what was wrong. The truth is that he did not really teach this book; I began to solve the work, and many were the complicated figures of which he had no knowledge until I presented them to him, and made him understand them. Then al-Natili took leave of me, setting out for Gurganj. "

Possibly al-Natili couldn't bear being in the same town any longer! Ibn Sina was extraordinarily intelligent and he was well aware of his superiority. But natural gifts are nothing without hard work, and the young boy worked exceptionally hard at his studies. Possibly he was also giving thought as to how he was going to earn a living as an adult, for Ibn Sina then went on to study the most practical of the sciences: medicine.

In his own words

" Next I desired to study medicine, and proceeded to read all the books that have been written on this

*subject. Medicine is not a difficult science, and naturally
I excelled in it in a very short time, so that qualified
physicians began to read medicine with me. I also
undertook to treat the sick, and methods of treatment
derived from practical experience revealed themselves
to me such as baffle description.* **99**

As can be seen, Ibn Sina did not lack for confidence. Not
many sixteen-year-olds would feel qualified to practise as
a doctor. Having mastered medicine, the young prodigy

Two doctors
preparing
medicine from
an Arabic
translation
of an ancient
Greek medical
encyclopedia.

The Kalyan Minaret, Bukhara, built in the 12th Century CE.

returned to studying logic and philosophy. For the next eighteen months he immersed himself in books, such that "during this time, I never slept a night through nor did I do anything but study during the day". To understand what he was studying, Ibn Sina broke each philosophical argument down into its separate parts and wrote them down in files. He then thought and pondered on the problem until he understood it completely.

If understanding proved difficult, Ibn Sina would visit the mosque and pray to God for insight. On other occasions, the answers to questions he was pondering would come to him in dreams.

This period of intensive study culminated with Ibn Sina mastering all the sciences to his satisfaction. He was, as far as he was concerned, the young man who knew everything. Well, almost everything.

In his own words

" By the time I reached my eighteenth birthday I had exhausted all these sciences. My memory for learning was at that period of my life better than it is now, but today I am more mature; apart from this my knowledge is exactly the same, nothing further having been added to my store since then. "

Man entering a
house of learning.

CHAPTER 3

The final science

There was one final branch of philosophy that Ibn Sina, despite his extraordinary accomplishments elsewhere, found completely mystifying: **metaphysics**. Metaphysics is the philosophy of *why* things are rather than *how* things are. The word itself means 'above physics' and was coined by the Greek philosopher Aristotle. Aristotle wrote his book, *Physics*, which deals with the natural world and how it behaves, and then went on to write *Metaphysics*, on why the world is as it is. Ibn Sina had a copy but could not make head or tail of it.

In his own words

❝ I read the Metaphysics, but did not understand its contents and was baffled by the author's intention; I read it over forty times until I had the text by heart. Even then I did not understand it or what the author meant, and I despaired. ❞

However, help came to the perplexed student in the shape of a Bukhara bookseller eager to cut a deal, "Buy this book from me; it is cheap, and I will sell it to you for four dirhams. The owner is in need of the money." So Ibn Sina bought the book – four dirhams was very cheap for a book at the time – and it provided him with the key to understanding Aristotle's book. Ibn Sina was so pleased that the next day he "gave many alms to the poor in thanks to God".

The little book that provided Ibn Sina with the key to metaphysics was called *On the Objects of Metaphysics*

by al-Farabi, the first great Muslim philosopher to attempt to integrate Greek thought into a Muslim context. Farabi argued that there are three sciences: physics, mathematics and metaphysics. Physics is the science of bodies and how they change; mathematics deals with the abstract characteristics of these bodies; while metaphysics deals with being as such, with what it is that provides the reality of things, their character, their kinds and

Modern statue of al-Farabi at Kozha Akhmed Yasaui, Kazakhstan.

their nature. This understanding, so hard won, was to prove crucial in Ibn Sina's later philosophical thought and writings.

For Ibn Sina, faith was profoundly intellectual. God was only perceptible by the intellect and thus the highest human function is the intellect. By the rigorous application of reasoning, Ibn Sina believed it was possible for a man like himself to understand the structure of reality as it flowed from its source, God. So what a

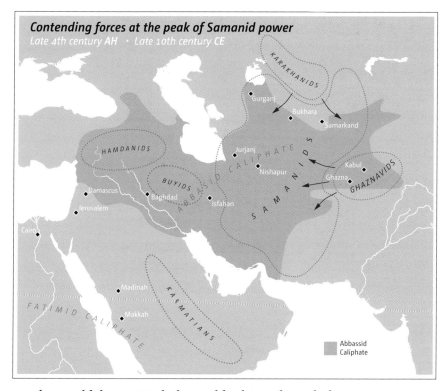

Contending forces at the peak of Samanid power
Late 4th century AH · Late 10th century CE

prophet could do intuitively, he could achieve through the
application of his intelligence.

Despite all his study, there were in fact still some things
Ibn Sina didn't know, but this was more the result of a lack
of books than a lack of application. Although Bukhara
was a cultured city with many scholars and rulers who
supported learning, books were still scarce and expensive,
since each had to be written and bound by hand. A library
was a rare and jealously guarded treasure – people could
not just wander in from the street and start to read. But for
a man as hungry for knowledge as Ibn Sina, there

The Samanid Mansur succeeds his father Nuh in 961 CE.

The Samanids

Arab Muslim armies invaded Persia in the seventh century and effectively destroyed the Sassanid Dynasty that had ruled there for over 400 years. The conquest was completed by 651. However, some of the aristocratic families of the old regime fled into Central Asia. These families began to carve out kingdoms among the perpetually fighting nomadic tribes that lived in the region. A nobleman of one of the old Persian families named Saman Khuda emerged a century and a half later to found a new kingdom. His son, Asad, took over after him and the Caliph Al-Mamun in Baghdad appointed Asad's sons as amirs of the region. Thus the Samanid dynasty was officially installed as rulers of the lands that today take in Afghanistan, the eastern half of Iran, and most of the Central Asian republics of Turkmenistan, Uzbekistan, Tajikistan and Kyrgyzstan.

Although now faithful Sunni Muslims – the dynasty's founder, Saman Khuda, had converted to Islam from **Zoroastrianism**, the old religion of Persia – the Samanids were intensely proud of their Persian identity. They did much to revive the Persian language and culture, declaring famously that "here, in this region, the language is Persian, and the kings of this realm are Persian kings".

By the time Ibn Sina came to live in Bukhara, the power of the Samanids was crumbling and he would live to see the first Persian realm since the Arab conquest utterly overthrown.

was one resource in his home city that must have been as tantalising as an oasis in a desert – the library of the Samanids, the rulers of Bukhara.

It was not Ibn Sina's thirst for knowledge but his skill as a doctor that bought him entry to the library in Bukhara. The ruling amir, Nuh ibn Mansur, had fallen seriously ill with a diarrhoeal infection and none of the doctors at court could cure him. However, the fame of the teenage medic was spreading and he was summoned to court. Ibn Sina cemented his reputation as the boy wonder by curing the amir. The gratitude of a prince is too valuable to waste, and when Ibn Sina was asked what gift he would like in return for saving the amir's life, he did not hesitate. Although he could have asked for gold and jewels, or a high position at court, he asked instead to be able to read the amir's books.

The Samanids were great patrons of learning, and at Bukhara they had assembled a library that was said to contain as many books as the great library in Baghdad. Ibn Sina's wonder at what he saw when the doors were opened to him is still obvious many years later when he recalled the event.

In his own words

" *I entered a mansion with many chambers, each chamber having chests of books piled one upon another. In one apartment were books on language and poetry, in another law, and so on; each apartment was set aside for books on a single science. I glanced through the catalogue of the works of the ancient Greeks, and asked* *for those which I required; and I saw books whose very names are as yet unknown to many – works which I had never seen before and have not seen since.* **"**

For the young scholar, it was like entering Aladdin's cave. Ibn Sina made full use of his access to these books, taking notes on what he read and filling his mind and memory with knowledge. And it was just as well he did, for not long afterwards the building went up in flames and the great library of Bukhara and its accumulated knowledge was lost. Ibn Sina's enemies swiftly put the blame on the young man, claiming that he had set fire to the library himself "so that he could attribute the contents of those books to himself", that is, pass off as his own ideas what he had first read in the lost library of Bukhara. There is no evidence for these claims, but flung mud does tend to stick, and Ibn Sina would always have to contend with these and other slanders throughout his life.

Quite why Ibn Sina had so many enemies is an interesting question. Jealousy must have played a part, for he really was the most intelligent and learned man of his time. It must have been galling for those who had studied for years to be surpassed by this young know-it-all who knew he was clever and saw no point in hiding it.

However, another reason for the attacks on him may have been his family. Ibn Sina's father and brother may have hosted Ismaili agents, and were suspected of being Ismailis themselves. As a member of the same family, and despite protestations that he had not accepted the Ismaili message, it was straightforward for an enemy to use the paranoid atmosphere of the time against Ibn Sina. Accusations of heresy (*bad-din*, literally, being of evil religion) were made against Ibn Sina in his own lifetime, and repeated after his death.

These accusations would have mattered little if Ibn Sina could have settled to a scholarly life at the court of the Samanid amir, Nuh ibn Mansur, whom he had cured and to whom he had dedicated his first book, written when he was seventeen. But all that was about to change.

Mud structures at Ayaz Kala, a site on
the Khwarezm plains near Gurganj .

CHAPTER 4

The wandering scholar

Ibn Sina's father, the man who had done more than anyone else to foster Ibn Sina's learning, died when his son was twenty-two. The brilliant young man was immediately given a government post, which may have been his father's old job of governor of Kharmaythan. Thus Ibn Sina had already assumed the two public roles through which he would earn his living through his adult life: as doctor to princes and amirs (as well as to ordinary people, whom he normally treated for free) and as what was basically an early form of civil servant, administering regions or government departments for his amir. It's highly likely that this is where he would have stayed but, as Ibn Sina delicately puts it in his autobiography, he "was obliged to move from Bukhara to Gurganj".

The Samanid amir who was Ibn Sina's patron, Nuh ibn Mansur, ruled from 976 to 997. After his death the leaders of the nomadic tribesmen who commanded the armies guarding the Samanid Dynasty had become increasingly assertive as the central power declined. Nuh ibn Mansur's relatives and the Samanid generals fell to warring over the succession. This was bad enough, but the rivals made the mistake of calling in the support of their increasingly restive vassals. These supposed allies looked around, saw the weakened state of the Samanid Dynasty but its still great wealth, and decided to help themselves. Soon Turkic warlords were setting up kingdoms out of the dismembered remains of the Samanid Dynasty.

Ibn Sina wished to avoid serving these new Turkic lords. This decision was probably based on a preference for a Persian court, as well a hard-headed assessment that he would be less able to continue his philosophical investigations and unorthodox lifestyle at their more religiously rigorous courts.

So, sometime around 1002, Ibn Sina left Bukhara. He does not mention any companions, but it is likely that his brother accompanied him, no doubt with attendant servants and slaves. Ibn Sina went north east, to Gurganj, a city on the banks of the River Oxus, south of the land-locked Aral Sea. The journey was long, over 500 kilometres (300 miles), through what is even today a rugged landscape. In Gurganj he stayed for over ten years. Although it was to be one of the longest stops on his expeditions around central Asia, Ibn Sina says little of his time there. The **vizier**, "an amateur of the sciences" according to Ibn Sina, presented the young man to the ruling amir, Ali ibn Mamun, as a religious lawyer, a status

The Turkic peoples

The Turkic peoples, who include the Turks of modern Turkey but also many other populations across Asia as far east as China, speak languages that are related to each other. They were a nomadic, pastoral people, originally from the steppes of Central Asia. Little is known of their early history, but under various leaders the Turkic peoples moved both west and east. The Seljuq branch of the Turkic peoples moved west and, under Alp Arslan, defeated the Byzantine Empire and opened Anatolia (now Turkey) to Turkic settlement. Other Turkic peoples include the Uzbeks of Uzbekistan and the Kazakhs of Kazakhstan.

indicated by the clothes Ibn Sina wore when he went to see the amir, namely a scarf and chinwrap. The amir bestowed an "amply sufficient" salary on the visitor but beyond that Ibn Sina says nothing.

However, the amir, Ali ibn Mamun, kept a scholarly court, and it is likely that here Ibn Sina met one of the other great figures of Islamic intellectual history: al-Biruni. Remarkably, their correspondence has been preserved. Al-Biruni posed the younger man eighteen questions on various topics, such as why do the planets and moon not fall from the sky and how do the rays of the sun produce warmth when they have no substance. These questions would nowadays be regarded as problems for science, but in this age they were regarded as metaphysical, and thus to be solved through the application of reason alone, rather than through experiment and reason.

Ibn Sina answered all the questions carefully, but al-Biruni was not satisfied, and sought further clarification as well as raising objections. The correspondence grew increasingly heated as the two geniuses sparred intellectually.

Al-Biruni: Why did Aristotle consider the views of the ancients and predecessors concerning the heaven and their finding [the celestial bodies] to be just as how he found them to be, a strong argument for immutability and perpetuity of the heaven? Anyone who is not stubborn and does not insist on falsehood would agree that this is not a known [fact].

Ibn Sina: You should know that [Aristotle] did not give

[the views of the ancients] as an evidence; it was only something that came by way of speech which he mentioned at two places… [You may have derived your arguments] from Muhammad ibn Zakariyyab al-Razi, who meddles in metaphysics and exceeds his competence. He should have remained confined to surgery and to urine and stool testing – indeed he exposed himself and showed his ignorance in these matters… And as for your saying, "anyone who is not stubborn and who does not insist on falsehood", this is an ugly and rude insult – either you comprehended the saying of Aristotle in this matter or you did not. If you did not, your belittling of someone who said something beyond your grasp is inappropriate. And if you did understand, your comprehension of the meaning should have prevented you from dragging in this quarrel; for your pursuit of what your intelligence prevents you from pursuing is inappropriate.

Finally and rather uncharacteristically, Ibn Sina gave up trying to convince al-Biruni he was right and had one of his best students continue the correspondence on his behalf. The student, of course, had no doubt who was correct: "As for your response to the Wise One… I do not think it was correct, and it would have been better had you worded your comment more appropriately."

Ibn Sina would probably have been content to spend the rest of his life in Gurganj in this atmosphere of brilliant intellectual debate and with sufficient material support from the amir to ensure a comfortable life. But it may have been necessity that drove him from the city. The name of that necessity would have been Mahmud of Ghazna.

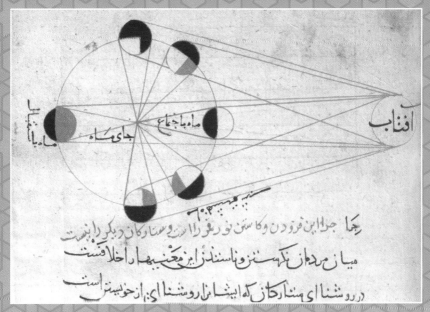

Different phases of a lunar eclipse by al-Biruni.

Al-Biruni

Abu Muhammad al-Biruni (973-1048) was a mathematician and astronomer, who also made large contributions to fields as diverse as comparative religion, history and geology. Al-Biruni was a Persian and came from a poor family so it was vital that he find a rich patron to support him in his studies. War drove him him hither and thither for a number of years, and he endured considerable poverty, until he made his way to the court of Ali ibn Mamun in Gurganj. He spent many productive years there, but when a more powerful prince, Mahmud of Ghazna, ordered Ali ibn Mamun to send him his best scholars, al-Biruni decided to answer the summons. He spent the remainder of his life at the court of Mahmud in Afghanistan, frequently accompanying his lord on his raids into India and thus acquiring the material to write his *History of India* (*Ta'rikh al-Hind*).

Although Ibn Sina never met him, Mahmud of Ghazna probably had a greater impact on his life than anyone else, for the scholar spent many years on the run from this notoriously acquisitive warlord.

Warlords came to power by the sword, but to maintain their thrones they had to be seen to be legitimate rulers. One way of doing this was to sponsor scholars and artists, and the more brilliant and talented the better. So kings and princes competed to acquire the greatest minds of the day and, as the story goes, Ibn Sina was high on the wish list for Mahmud of Ghazna. There were many other noted scholars and artists in Gurganj, including al-Biruni, and the amir of Gurganj did not have the strength to oppose Mahmud when he 'requested' that these intellectuals

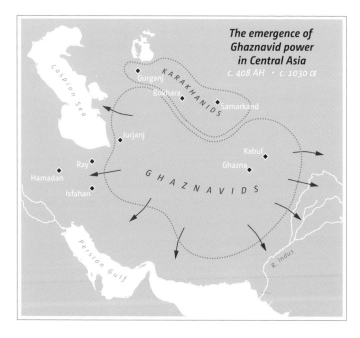

The emergence of Ghaznavid power in Central Asia
c. 408 AH · c. 1030 CE

The Ghaznavids

The Samanids employed slave soldiers from the nomadic tribes of central Asia. Gradually these slaves realised that, since they ran the army, real power lay with them, and not their masters. Slave generals took command of their troops and started to set themselves up as independent rulers. The most important among these was the great grandfather of Sultan Mahmud, who took the city of Ghazna in modern-day Afghanistan for his own. As the strength of this dynasty increased, that of the Samanids decreased, until Mahmud conquered much of the lands previously ruled by the Samanids. The Ghaznavids, as they were called, had come a long way from their origins as warlords.

Mahmud of Ghazna, the first independent Ghaznavid ruler, receiving a richly decorated robe of honor from the Abbasid caliph.

Ibn Sina
surrounded by
his students.

should relocate to Ghazna. However, the amir warned Ibn Sina and the others of the summons, allowing them the chance to stay or flee. In the end, most of them, including al-Biruni, decided to throw in their lot with Sultan Mahmud, prospering to various degrees. But Ibn Sina was determined to evade Mahmud's summons.

The reasons for his decision are clear enough – although he makes no mention of Mahmud in his autobiography. First, Mahmud was Turkic, and Ibn Sina always preferred the courts of Persian princes. But, more importantly, Mahmud of Ghazna was fiercely orthodox in religion and a determined opponent of the Ismailis. With Ibn Sina's family background, and the intrigues and plotting that went on at a court, it would have been tantamount to suicide to accept Mahmud's invitation. Nor was it likely that a self-styled defender of the faith would have much truck with either Ibn Sina's ideas or his lifestyle.

So, in 1012, Ibn Sina fled Gurganj with another refugee from the court in Gurganj, a Christian artist named Abu

Sahl. They were making for Abu Sahl's home, the city of Jurjanj (now called Gorgan, in Iran), which lies at the south-east corner of the Caspian Sea. The amir of that land, a man named Qabus ibn Vushmagir (c.978-1012), had been an ally of the Samanids and was himself a noted poet in Persian and Arabic.

One source states that when Mahmud of Ghazna heard that Ibn Sina had slipped from his grasp, he ordered that a portrait be painted of the fugitive, copied many times over and then sent out over his realm with accompanying orders that Ibn Sina be arrested and brought to him should he be identified. Ibn Sina and Abu Sahl were outlaws.

The journey was long and hard for the fugitives. They tried as best they could to avoid the territories ruled by Mahmud but, with a price on their heads, nowhere was safe. They made their way from village to village, trying to

Travellers by a campfire.

Al-Juzjani

Al-Juzjani writes the story of the rest of Ibn Sina's life. The young man had read the master's works and searched for him. When al-Juzjani found Ibn Sina, he became his friend, confidant and biographer, continuing the story of Ibn Sina's life to its end, for he accompanied him through all the years that followed. Al-Juzjani was devoted to his master, and determined that he should receive the recognition he believed he deserved. Al-Juzjani sat with his master every day, taking dictation, reading aloud to him and generally helping with his work. Ibn Sina, who was never one to underestimate his own value, must have been delighted. The transition from one voice to another in the story of Ibn Sina's life is marked by this verse of poetry:

I grew so big that no city could hold me
But my price went so high that every buyer has sold me.

Al-Juzjani was saying that the physician philosopher was too big a man for the world in which he lived. Since Ibn Sina quotes it as the final remark of his own section of his biography, he must have agreed with the sentiments.

keep ahead of the pursuit, but out in the open in the harsh plains, Ibn Sina and his companion were caught by a huge sand storm. Unable to see more than a few feet, with their cloaks over their heads to protect their eyes and throats from the sand, the men attempted to sit out the storm. When it finally lifted, Abu Sahl was dead. Distraught and desperate, Ibn Sina struggled on to Jurjanj. However, he arrived only to discover that his supposed protector and host had not been able to protect himself.

" My entire purpose was to come to the Amir Qabus; but it happened meanwhile that Qabus was taken and imprisoned in a fortress, where he died. "

To make matters worse, the son of Qabus, who took over as amir, then married one of Mahmud of Ghazna's daughters. Jurjanj was no longer the refuge Ibn Sina had hoped to find. It was time to move on. Ibn Sina headed north to Dihistan, but all the travelling took its toll and he fell very ill there. When Ibn Sina finally recovered he returned south, to the town he had left before, Jurjanj. And there he met the other person who was to prove most important in his life, his friend, pupil and disciple, Abu Ubayd al-Juzjani.

Ibn Sina at the bedside of an ailing young nobleman.

CHAPTER 5

On the road again

Although Ibn Sina's time in Jurjanj was marked by disappointment, it was while he was living in the city that the philosopher began writing the medical textbook that would prove probably his most influential legacy: the *Canon of Medicine*. The constant travelling would have made writing difficult if not impossible for most people, but Ibn Sina took it in his stride. Because of his extraordinary, and highly trained, memory, he did not need to have books available for reference – he carried them in his head. Nor did the disruption of travelling break his concentration. He would often dictate to al-Juzjani or some other scribe the text of his newest work while they rode along.

The first stop for Ibn Sina and his faithful companion al-Juzjani on their peregrinations was Ray, which lies on the outskirts of the present-day capital of Iran, Tehran. The city was the richest in northern Persia, due to its position on one of the major trade routes from central Asia to Iraq. The city was ancient – archaeologists have found settlements there dating to the third millennium BCE – and it is mentioned in the Bible and the Avesta, the sacred texts of the Zoroastrian religion. Under Muslim rule it grew in importance so much that it rivalled

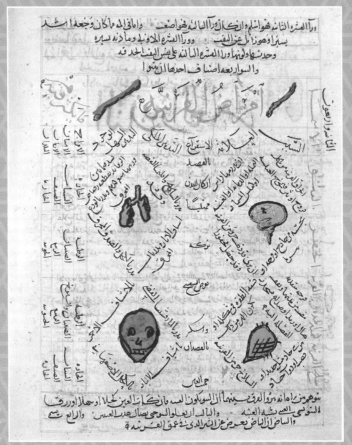

Page from a 14th
Century copy of the
Canon of Medicine.

The Canon of Medicine

Medical knowledge at the time of Ibn Sina mainly came from the
study of the writing of ancient Greek and Roman writers. Of these,
there was one who was the supreme authority on medical matters:
Claudius Galen (c129-c199). Galen was a Greek who served as
physician to five Roman emperors. He wrote a vast amount on
medicine and philosophy and his reputation as the greatest doctor
in history survived for a thousand years after his death. Apart from

them both being the best physicians of their respective eras, Galen shared another trait with Ibn Sina. He had a very high opinion of himself, "I have done as much for medicine as Trajan did for the Roman Empire when he built roads and bridges. It is I, and I alone, who have revealed the true path of medicine. It must be admitted that Hippocrates already staked out this path ... but I have made it passable." But there were other medical authorities, plus the accumulated practical knowledge of some 800 years of medical practice, so Ibn Sina set about writing what was to become the most important medical textbook of his time – and a long time to come. The *Canon* is half a million words long, and in its many books it examines medical knowledge from the Greeks through to Ibn Sina's own time. But Ibn Sina was not content merely to report what others had said. After all, he had many years' experience as a doctor himself and, besides, "medicine is not one of the difficult sciences". So the *Canon* contains much of the knowledge that Ibn Sina had gained for himself.

Among the many advances it contained was the idea that diseases can be contagious; that quarantine can help stop the spread of infectious diseases; and that soil and water can both be channels for the spread of diseases.

But perhaps more important than any one insight was Ibn Sina's insistence on the use of evidence in medicine, rather than relying on the word of doctors from the past. This is shown particularly in Ibn Sina's book on drugs, where he laid out specific and accurate rules for testing drugs to determine whether and how they work. These rules are the foundation for medical drug trials today. Even something as straightforward as taking a patient's pulse by holding the wrist goes back to Ibn Sina's writing in the *Canon*.

So great was the impact of the *Canon* that it remained a standard medical textbook for hundreds of years. When it had been translated into Latin in the twelfth century, it was the main textbook used in European universities for training doctors for over half a millennium.

Baghdad and Damascus as a centre of Islamic civilisation, with buildings shimmering with blue faience (glazed earthenware).

One of the main ways for a visiting scholar or jurist to gain entry to a royal court, and the patronage it offered, was through letters of introduction. Ibn Sina carried many. But it was through his medical skills that Ibn Sina found a way into the royal circle.

The ruler of Ray, Majd al-Dawla, had inherited the throne as a four-year-old child. To protect her son from the machinations of ambitious relatives and rivals, his formidable mother took over running the country. The trouble for Majd al-Dawla was that, as he reached maturity, his mother, who was known as al-Saiyyida (the Lady), refused to give up her authority to her son. Instead, she kept him quiet in the **harem**. Amidst a fog of pleasure the young man fell into a deep depression. Ibn Sina treated the young man and cured him. His entry to Ray's elite was assured but upon trying to help the son again – arguing to al-Saiyyida that Majd al-Dawla should be allowed to assume the power that his position promised – Ibn Sina was forced to leave Ray two years later.

This principled stand on behalf of the weaker party counteracts the easily gained impression that Ibn Sina always looked after his own interests first. But, principles aside, the increasing interest of his old enemy, Mahmud of Ghazna, in acquiring the city of Ray may also have persuaded him it was time to leave.

Ibn Sina's next stop was Hamadan, the city ruled by the

The Lady and Mahmud

The wealth of Ray came to the notice of Ibn Sina's nemesis, Mahmud of Ghazna, and this most rapacious of warlords moved towards the city. However, al-Saiyyida chose to meet him with words, rather than weapons. Al-Saiyyida wrote to Mahmud, saying:

> As long as my husband was alive, I lived in fear that thoughts of conquering Ray would come into your head, but since he died my heart is freed of that disquiet. For I said to myself, "Sultan Mahmud is a reasonable monarch; he knows that a ruler like himself should not make war against a woman like me." But should you come, God knows I will not run. For there can be but two outcomes, since one army must be beaten. If it is mine that carries the day, I shall write to the entire world that I have broken Sultan Mahmud, who broke a hundred kings ... But if it is you who are the victor, what will you write? That you have broken the power of a woman?

This formidable lady held off Mahmud until her death in 1028. But after she died, Majd al-Dawla couldn't control his soldiers and made the mistake of calling on Mahmud for help. Mahmud promptly helped himself to the city, taking Majd al-Dawla prisoner and proving the mother's low estimation of her son's abilities was all too accurate.

more capable brother of Majd al-Dawla, Shams al-Dawla. This ancient city lay 280 kilometres (175 miles) west of Ray. Ibn Sina's medical skills again provided him with an entry to the royal circle, as Shams al-Dawla was suffering from a bowel disease and Ibn Sina cured him. The two men became friends and Shams al-Dawla, seeing the unique range of abilities of his physician, appointed him his vizier. The power of a vizier was potentially very great, and surely now any enemies could not move against him. However, Ibn Sina was to have a rough introduction to the world of politics.

In Al-Jujzani's words

" *The army conspired against him, fearing for themselves on his account; they surrounded his house, hauled him off to prison, pillaged his belongings, and took all that he possessed. They even demanded of the Amir that he should put him to death.* "

Bird's eye view of the city of Hamadan.

Such behaviour was typical of the armies of the time and a prudent ruler worked to mollify their demands rather than simply refusing them; anger against a vizier could easily transform into plots against an amir. Shams al-Dawla publicly banished Ibn Sina, but the banishment appears to have been made in agreement with Ibn Sina, for the philosopher simply hid in a friend's house for a month or so while the grievances of the army cooled down. A further attack of the debilitating bowel disease led to Ibn Sina being called out of hiding and to the amir's bedside. With Shams al-Dawla restored to health, Ibn Sina was restored to power, reassuming the post of vizier.

This period in Hamadan, which lasted from 1015 to 1024, was to prove one of the most productive of Ibn Sina's life. He worked hard and he entertained lavishly. To keep up with all his commitments, Ibn Sina got up before dawn each day, worked on the book he was writing, and then called in his pupils and together they read some pages from his books. Then it was time for his official work. Ibn Sina went to court and, taking his official divan – officials of the time received visitors and supplicants reclining on a divan – he dealt with all the matters of business that were part of the everyday duties of a vizier. At lunch time, Ibn Sina went home and entertained guests. Following the siesta through the heat of the day, it was back to court and a private audience with the amir to discuss the affairs of state. But a day that began before dawn continued on into the night.

In Al-Jujzani's words

" Every night students gathered in his house, and by turns I would read the Kitab al-Shifa (Book of Healing) and another the Canon. When we had finished the allotted portion the various musicians would enter ... and so we occupied ourselves. The studying was done by night because during the day his attendance upon the amir left him no spare time. "

Such a lifestyle, as a Muslim, brought gossip and rumour but, wielding the power of a vizier, Ibn Sina could afford to disregard popular opinion. Or he could do so for as long as the amir supported him.

In 1021, Shams al-Dawla died from a recurrence of the

bowel complaint that had plagued his life. His son, Sama al-Dawla, took over as amir. Although the new amir asked Ibn Sina to continue as vizier, the wary scholar appears to have decided that, with his old patron dead, Hamadan was no longer the sanctuary it had once appeared to be. So, while he played for time, Ibn Sina wrote to the ruler of Isfahan, 380 kilometres (235 miles) south east, seeking a post at his court. The ruler of Isfahan was Ala al-Dawla, the cousin of al-Saiyyida, the Lady of Ray.

Secret correspondence with a rival ruler is a dangerous game and Ibn Sina decided that it might be better to lie low while he waited for a reply. He went into hiding, staying at the house of a pharmacist friend.

Freed from the demands of court, Ibn Sina had plenty of time to write, and he took full advantage of the opportunity. Writing some fifty pages a day, he began work on *The Book of Healing* (*Kitab al-Shifa*) which, despite its title, doesn't say much about medicine. In fact, it's an encyclopaedia of science and philosophy. It deals with astronomy, geology, physics and psychology on the science side, and logic and metaphysics for philosophy. As with the *Canon*, Ibn Sina surveyed the existing state of each discipline, pointed out what he thought valuable about it, and then went on to add his own insights and thoughts.

However, the news leaked that Ibn Sina had been corresponding with the ruler of Isfahan. This was particularly unfortunate, as Ala al-Dawla was now at war with Sama al-Dawla. Some enemies of Ibn Sina – and he was never short of those – informed Sama al-Dawla where he was hiding. Ibn Sina was captured and dragged off to a castle some 55 miles from Hamadan. Things did not look bright for the man who knew everything. This is reflected in a little poem Ibn Sina wrote about his imprisonment.

In his own words

" That I go in you see, so that's without doubt.
What's uncertain is whether I ever come out. "

As ever, Ibn Sina used his time in prison productively, writing three books while he was held captive. Although the couplet quoted above hints at doubt and misery, the energy that fired Ibn Sina's life and thought ensured that he never succumbed to despair. And in the war between the princes, Ala al-Dawla proved a better general than Sama al-Dawla. Ironically, the defeated amir, Sama al-Dawla, took refuge in the castle where he was holding Ibn Sina prisoner. When Ala al-Dawla returned to Isfahan, Sama al-Dawla cautiously emerged from the castle, taking Ibn Sina with him back to Hamadan. Sama al-Dawla promised Ibn Sina all sorts of rewards if he stayed. However, the scholar decided not to stay in the city of the man who had held him prisoner for four months. So, in 1024, and disguised as **Sufis**, Ibn Sina, his faithful disciple al-Juzjani, his brother Mahmud and two slaves slipped out of the city, heading for Isfahan.

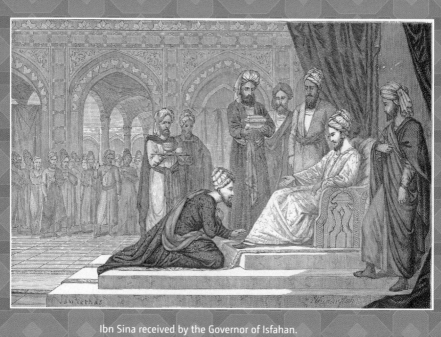

Ibn Sina received by the Governor of Isfahan.

CHAPTER 6

Safe haven

No lengthy journey at that time was easy. Ibn Sina and his companions faced an arduous trip but at least this time no one died. And when he at last arrived at the outskirts of Isfahan, he was met by courtiers of Ala al-Dawla "and clothing and fine horses were brought to him". Ibn Sina had arrived at a court where he was both valued and, finally he thought, safe from Mahmud of Ghazna. After all the journeys and escapes and travels of his life, Ibn Sina had come to the place that would be his home.

Ibn Sina was immensely grateful to Ala al-Dawla. In the introduction to a book he wrote for the amir, he expressed his thanks to the ruler for granting him "all his wishes, in security, and eminence and honour". Ibn Sina would remain at Ala al-Dawla's side for the rest of his life, through all the vicissitudes that the amir would face. At the previous courts where Ibn Sina had found employment and patronage, there is always the sense that the philosopher was looking after himself, and that if the going for his patron got tough, he would head for the exit. But this was not the case with Ala al-Dawla. The two men forged a deep and lasting friendship, based on mutual respect and shared intellectual interests. If Ala al-Dawla went down, Ibn Sina would go with him. But the trials

A discussion of intellectuals.

came later. For the first five years in Isfahan, Ibn Sina must have felt he was back in an environment as conducive to learning and conversation as Bukhara under the Samanids.

In al-Jujzani's words

" *Ala al-Dawla appointed every Friday night a meeting for learned discussion before him, to be attended by all the scholars according to their various degrees, the master among them; in these gatherings he proved himself quite supreme and unrivalled in every branch of learning.* "

Ibn Sina must have thoroughly enjoyed these gatherings. At last he was with men who were, if not his equals intellectually, at least able to appreciate what he was saying. Ibn Sina even contributed to discussions in **philology**. But one of the other scholars, a man named Abu Mansur, protested, "You are a philosopher and a physician. You have not learned enough about philology for us to believe what you say on the subject."

An observatory in Maragha, Persia.

Ibn Sina was not the sort of individual to accept this. But it was true, he really did not know very much about philology. So he set about changing that. He studied the Arabic language for three years.

Once Ibn Sina had mastered philology, he decided it was time to play a little joke on Abu Mansur. He wrote three poems, full of old and obscure words, and three little books, each in the style of a different writer. He then had the books made to look as if they were old, and presented them all to Abu Mansur. When the philologist was unable to explain the language in them, Ibn Sina, who after all had written them in the first place, explained what they meant. Abu Mansur finally caught on to the joke and apologised to Ibn Sina, who accepted gracefully.

At the request of the amir, Ibn Sina created an

observatory to make astronomical observations, designing some of the equipment himself. From here, Ibn Sina observed the transit of Venus, that is the passage of the planet between sun and earth, with Venus appearing as a black disc on the face of the sun. More philosophical works also flowed from his pen and also answers to objections that other scholars raised. One group of scholars sent a representative to Isfahan with a number of questions and objections to Ibn Sina's work. Once Ibn Sina had read their letter, he asked the faithful al-Juzjani to bring him 50 sheets of paper.

In al-Jujzani's words

" *We prayed the evening prayer; candles were brought, and the Master ... commenced to answer the questions that had been propounded to him .... In the morning a knock came at the door, and there was the Master's messenger summoning me. I found him at his prayers, and before him the answers completed. 'Take them to our questioner and tell him I made haste to reply so that the post-messenger might not be delayed.'* "

But the freedom Ibn Sina had found at Ala al-Dawla's court was not to last. His old nemesis was about to make his last years miserable. In 1029, Mahmud of Ghazna conquered the city of Ray after the Lady died. His armies destroyed the magnificent library and burned its books "at the feet of the corpses of the Ismailis, **Rafidis**, philosophers and other unbelievers that hung from the trees". Mahmud put his son, Masud, in charge of the campaign, and he marched south against Isfahan. Masud

Mahmud of Ghazna's victory column, Ghazni, Afghanistan.

was as capable a general as his father, and Ala al-Dawla was forced to retreat. In the general confusion, Ibn Sina's luggage was lost, and the manuscript of some of his works lost.

However, there came a temporary respite. Mahmud of Ghazna died. Ibn Sina's nemesis, the man who had caused him to flee across the plains of Central Asia and Persia, was out of the picture and his son, Masud, rushed back home to fight it out with his brothers for the throne. This was quite normal after the death of a strong ruler. The rival sons, and sometimes generals if they could command a following, would generally settle their differences on the battlefield. It was a brutal struggle for survival. The loser was not always put to death, but to ensure any defeated claimants for the throne could not press their claim anew, the victor would blind his defeated brothers.

Sadly for Ala al-Dawla and Ibn Sina, Masud won the battle. With his throne secure, Masud could not allow Ala al-Dawla to remain defiant and he returned repeatedly to Isfahan over the next few years, capturing the city time and again. But Ala al-Dawla would not submit. And, for the only time in his life, Ibn Sina did not abandon his patron, even when Ala al-Dawla was repeatedly defeated by Masud. Instead, he accompanied his ruler on desperate retreats, then returned with him as business elsewhere forced Masud to withdraw, allowing Ala al-Dawla to reclaim his city.

The start of Ibn Sina's decline began in 1034. Masud's army had captured Isfahan again, and Ala al-Dawla was

Mahmud of Ghazna attacks a fortress.

75

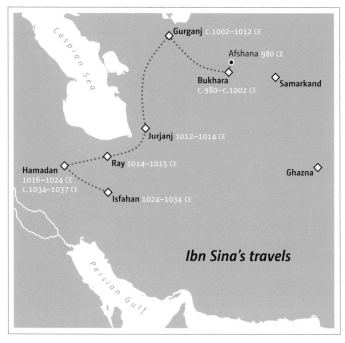

Caspian Sea

Gurganj c.1002–1012 CE

Afshana 980 CE

Bukhara c.980–c.1002 CE

Samarkand

Jurjanj 1012–1014 CE

Ray 1014–1015 CE

Hamadan 1016–1024 CE c.1034–1037 CE

Ghazna

Isfahan 1024–1034 CE

Persian Gulf

Ibn Sina's travels

in retreat. But the master physician fell seriously ill with some form of bowel disease. If he was not to be left behind and captured by Masud's troops, Ibn Sina had to cure himself. In the rush, he overdid the cure, causing an open wound that had no time to heal. Ibn Sina began to suffer from seizures and when he tried to treat those, the doctor he asked to administer the cure overdosed him.

To make matters worse, a slave mixed a large amount of opium into the drugs that Ibn Sina had prescribed himself to treat his seizures. According to al-Juzjani, the slave did this because he had stolen money from his master and, to escape punishment, he wanted to dispose of his master before his theft could be discovered. Although al-Juzjani does not tell us what happened to the slave, Ibn Sina's extraordinary vigour was enough to overcome these twin overdoses.

However, weakened and amid the rigours of the continuing war against Masud, Ibn Sina's body started to break down completely. Ibn Sina, the greatest doctor of his age, knew well that in the end all medicine is a long struggle against inevitable defeat.

In his own words

" *The governor that used to rule my body is too weak to rule any longer. Treatment is of no further use.* "

Ibn Sina died in Hamadan, during Ramadan, in June or July 1037 CE /428 AH. He was fifty-seven.

Tomb of Ibn Sina, Hamadan, Iran.

CHAPTER 7

What was Ibn Sina like?

On an intellectual level, Ibn Sina's key characteristic, above even the brilliance of his mind, the sharpness of his insights and the retentiveness of his memory, was his energy. He continued working and thinking through the most trying circumstances, apparently finding a sanctuary in thinking on philosophical problems when on the march or, indeed, fleeing for his life.

But it was not his mind that was most immediately obvious to people meeting Ibn Sina for the first time. While there are no surviving contemporary portraits of him, a number of ancient sources testify to him being extraordinarily handsome, so much so that once, when in hiding, he was recognised in the **bazaar** purely on the basis of his good looks. So, in one sense, he really was the man with everything: intelligence, ability, looks. On the other hand, there is something intensely lonely about his life. Ibn Sina never married, and there are no records of his having any children, so he knew any legacy could only come through his work. It was expected and normal practice for a man to marry, so Ibn Sina's decision not to get married was unusual. It could not have been because of a lack of interest because his biographer, Al-Juzjani, candidly remarks that his master had very strong carnal appetites, so it was probably a life often lived on the run that led Ibn Sina to reject marriage and fatherhood for himself.

But Ibn Sina was no recluse. He loved company, conversation, music and song. By all accounts he was a brilliant conversationalist, able to illuminate any gathering with his knowledge. His wit was cutting, and his tongue must have left many an opponent feeling lacerated. As an example, he dismissed the philosophising of another famous physician/philosopher, Razi, as that of a man who should not have strayed from "testing stools and urine". People who wrote about him praised the mind, never the man.

However, there was a different side to him that emerged most clearly in his final years at the court of Ala al-Dawla. Before coming to Isfahan, there was always the sense that Ibn Sina used the princes and rulers he served entirely for his own ends, abandoning them without a second glance when trouble loomed. But Ibn Sina remained with Ala al-Dawla through thick and thin, through a series of military defeats that left the prince beaten but his will unbroken. Before his relationship with Ala al-Dawla, the threat of his nemesis, Mahmud of Ghazna, was enough to send Ibn Sina running, but for the final thirteen years of his life he hitched his fortunes completely to those of his prince, suggesting a deep personal friendship and devotion between them.

In Ala al-Dawla, Ibn Sina was fortunate in finding a patron who appreciated the remarkable man he had in

his employ. Although Ibn Sina did nothing to change his non-conformist lifestyle, with the amir's support he was safe from censure. The way Ibn Sina absolutely ignored the opinions of others suggests a man who may have taken some pleasure in outraging common opinion, yet despite the irregularities of his life, Ibn Sina certainly considered himself a Muslim, writing, "If I am a heretic, then there is not a single Muslim anywhere in the world." Al-Juzjani records his master saying the normal Muslim prayers at the appropriate times, and much of his philosophising was directed towards a rational understanding of the interaction between God and His creation. Indeed, so creative was Ibn Sina's philosophy that he anticipated one of the key modern philosophers,

Ibn Sina with the other medical experts Galenus and Hippocrates from a 15th Century French manuscript.

Descartes, in his analysis of consciousness as the basis of the proof of existence, an idea the Frenchman summed up in his aphorism, *cogito ergo sum* (I think therefore I am). This commitment to reason underlay the difficulties Ibn Sina had with religion: for him religion was a matter of reason rather than faith.

But this does not mean that God was not important to Ibn Sina – far from it. It was rather that he approached God as much through reason as through prayer. Indeed, he formulated a brilliant proof of the existence of God based on the idea that God is the sole necessary being that gives rise to all the other dependent levels of creation.

So dominant was Ibn Sina's thought that, when a hundred years later the theologian al-Ghazali set out to counter the arguments of philosophers, he based his rebuttal purely on Ibn Sina's work. For while Ibn Sina considered himself a practising Muslim, philosophical reasoning had led him to adopt a number of ideas that were contrary to the tenets of Islam, in particular, that the world was eternal and a rejection of bodily resurrection. Al-Ghazali wrote *The Incoherence of the Philosophers*, attempting to show the contradictions in Ibn Sina's thought, and within the Islamic world al-Ghazali certainly won the argument. Henceforth, philosophers had to accept the primacy of faith.

In the west, Ibn Sina was the first of the great Muslim philosophers to be widely read and his exposition of the works of Aristotle became a standard part of scholarly knowledge, to such an extent that the greatest of all

The Jameh Mosque of Isfahan, founded in the 8th Century CE.

medieval theologians, Thomas Aquinas, quotes him more than 400 times.

Indeed, in the range of his genius, the nearest Western equivalent is probably Leonardo da Vinci. While there

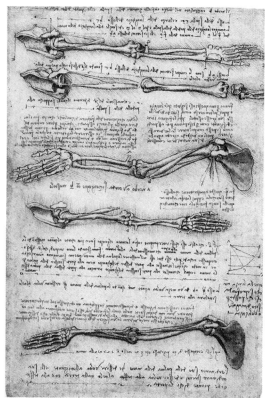

Anatomical studies by Leonardo da Vinci.

is no record of Ibn Sina painting or drawing (although if he ever had taken up the brush, no doubt his desire to excel would have ensured the odd masterpiece), like Leonardo, he investigated all branches of human knowledge and mastered most of them, from the practicalities of medicine to the abstruse thinking of philosophy. Such was his impact on the Muslim world that his like has not, to this day, been seen again.

For Ibn Sina, supreme happiness lay in the moment of insight that accompanies understanding. For him, that was the location of the most intimate possible encounter between the human and the divine, and he dedicated his life to pursuing such insight.

In his book, *Hints and Pointers*, Ibn Sina has this final piece of advice for all those who read his works.

In his own words

" Dear Brother, I've churned my best cream for you and fed you my finest dishes, words whipped from the froth of wisdom. Keep it safe from boors and ... any who

listen to the crowd, from renegade philosophers and the flies that buzz around them. But if you find someone you're sure is of good faith and upright living, who can withstand temptation and keep his sight fixed on the truth cheerfully and sincerely, give him what he needs from this, gradually, bit by bit, watching his reactions, and make him swear to God by oaths that cannot be broken that he will follow calmly where you lead him. But if you spread this knowledge around and waste it, may God judge between us. For God is the surest guarantor. **"**

Timeline

980 CE   Ibn Sina born in Afshana, near Bukhara, in present-day Uzbekistan.

997   Death of Nuh ibn Mansur, the amir of Bukhara.

c.1002   Ibn Sina leaves Bukhara and moves to Gurganj to join the court of the amir Ali ibn Mamun.

1012   Ibn Sina flees Gurganj to avoid the summons of Mahmud of Ghazna. (An alternative account tells us that Ibn Sina may have left Gurjanj around 1009 for other reasons.)

1013   Ibn Sina meets his pupil and biographer, Abu Ubayd al-Juzjani, in Jurjanj (now called Gorgan, in Iran).

c.1013   Ibn Sina begins to write the *Canon of Medicine*.

1014   Ibn Sina moves to Ray (near present-day Tehran) and accepts service at the court of Majd al-Dawla.

1015   Ibn Sina flees Ray and goes to Hamadan, ruled by Shams al-Dawla, the brother of Majd al-Dawla.

c.1016	Appointed vizier by Shams al-Dawla.
1021	Death of Shams al-Dawla. Ibn Sina starts looking for a safer position at a different court.
1023	Ibn Sina is imprisoned for four months.
1024	Ibn Sina and his companions leave Hamadan disguised as Sufis and make for Isfahan. In Isfahan, he enters the service of Ala al-Dawla.
1030	Death of Mahmud of Ghazna.
1032	Mahmud's son, Masud, begins to attack Ala al-Dawla.
1034	Ibn Sina falls ill when accompanying Ala al-Dawla on retreat from Isfahan.
1037	Ibn Sina dies in Hamadan.

Glossary

Amir   a governor or ruler of a territory, usually under the overlordship of a sultan.

Bazaar   a market place.

Dactylonomy   calculating using fingers and finger joints.

Fiqh   Islamic jurisprudence.

Harem   the part of a palace reserved strictly for the ruler's wives and concubines.

Ismailism   a sect of Shia Islam.

Metaphysics   the part of philosophy that investigates first principles, that is, a thing's meaning and structure.

Philology   the science of language, and especially how it developed historically.

Rafidi   another name for Shia Muslims, now usually derogatory.

Shari'ah   Islamic law, based on the precepts in the Qur'an and the words and actions of the Prophet Muhammad (*Sunnah*).

Sufi   a Muslim following Sufism, the mystical branch of the Islamic faith.

Sultan   the ruler of a state.

Sunnah   the practice and teachings of the Prophet Muhammad.

Vizier   the chief minister of the ruling amir or sultan. Viziers could sometimes be more powerful than the sultans in whose name they ruled.

Zoroastrianism   the ancient religion of Persia.

Bibliography

Afnan, Soheil M (1958). *Avicenna: His Life and Works.* Greenwood Press.

Al-Khalili, Jim (2010). *Pathfinders: The Golden Age of Arabic Science.* Penguin Books.

Arberry, Arthur J (1951). *Avicenna on Theology.* John Murray.

Berjak, Rafik and Iqbal, Muzaffar, translators (2003–2007). *Islam and Science.* Center for Islam and Science.

Gohlman, William E (1974). *The Life of Ibn Sina: A Critical Edition and Annotated Translation.* State University of New York Press

Goodman, Lenn E (2006). *Avicenna.* Cornell University Press.

Khan, Aisha (2006). *Avicenna (Ibn Sina): Muslim Physician and Philosopher of the Eleventh Century.* Rosen Publishing Group.

Masood, Ehsan (2009). *Science and Islam: A History.* Icon Books.

Nasr, Seyyed Hossein (1988). *Three Muslim Sages.* Suhail Academy.

Further reading

There are very few good introductions to the life and works of Ibn Sina, apart from those listed in the bibliography. However, one overview of his philosophical work and its influence is *Avicenna* (Great Medieval Thinkers) by Jon McGinnis, published by OUP USA. There is also an excellent, although long, translation of Ibn Sina's *Kitab al-Shifa*, called *The Metaphysics of the Healing*, published by the University of Chicago Press. The *Canon of Medicine* is available in a translation by Laleh Bakhtiar, published by Kazi Publications.

Since much of Ibn Sina's thought was an engagement with Aristotle, a good introduction to Aristotle will take you close to the centre of Ibn Sina's work. Try:

Adler, Mortimer J. (1992). *Aristotle for Everybody: Difficult Thought Made Easy*. Collier Paperbacks.

Aristotle (2004). *The Nicomachean Ethics*. Penguin.

The history of this period of contending empires is, frankly, confusing. A good place to start is with Kube Publishing's handsome volume, *A Journey Through Islamic History: A Timeline of Key Events*, by Yasminah Hashim and M.A.J. Beg.

Index

The author

Edoardo Albert is a London-based writer of Italian and Sri Lankan extraction. He specialises in religion, travel and archaeology, and gets up early in the morning (5am!) to write stories. To find out more about his work, visit **www.edoardoalbert.com**

Also available in the Concise Life series:

In this short biography you will discover
how Imam al-Ghazali (1058–1111 CE) rose
from his humble background as a fatherless
young boy to become the preeminent
Muslim scholar of the eleventh century and
a towering figure in the history of Islamic
thought. It also reveals why, after years
of success, he left behind his prestigious
teaching position and became a penniless
traveler trying to experience the peace of a
contented inner life.

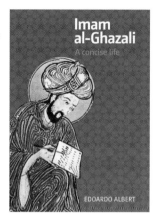

ISBN 978-1-84774-030-4